It's easy to have a WORM visit you

Advisory Editor

Caroline O'Hagan

Illustrations by

Judith Allan

LOTHROP, LEE & SHEPARD BOOKS
NEW YORK

An earthworm is a soft, crawly animal that lives under the ground, and if you would like to have a worm visit you, it is easy to catch one. Some kinds of worms make a cast, a little round squiggle of earth on the ground. If you see a worm-cast, you know there has been a worm burrowing away underground.

595
It's

4.95
1988-89

Discard

You can dig in the earth almost anywhere the soil is cool and moist and find an earthworm.

Before you look for your worm you should make a special place for it to stay in while it visits you. Get two sheets of Plexiglas or glass and three pieces of wood and make a tall, narrow box that you can see into. You can use a big jar but you will be able to see more if your worm's box is tall and narrow.

Now fill up the box with layers of different colored things like sand, earth, bonemeal, peat, or compost. Most important of all is a layer of earth with plenty of leaf mold in it, because this is what your worm eats.

Always keep your worm's box cool and moist — but don't make it too wet or your worm might drown.

Put your worm on top of its new home and have a good look at it. You will see that worms have no legs or feet or bones. If you wait for a minute or two you will see it begin to burrow.

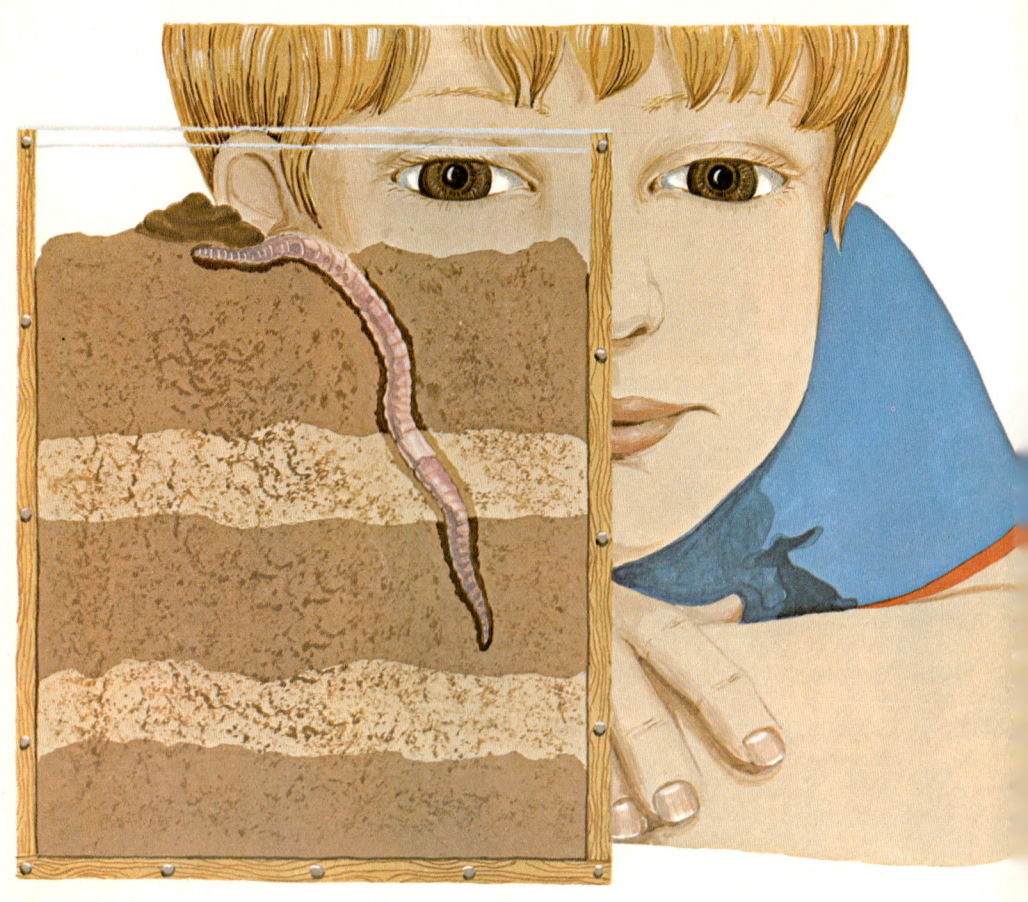

As your worm tunnels down, it sucks the earth in, digests what it needs, and leaves the rest behind. The earth it leaves behind is a worm-cast.

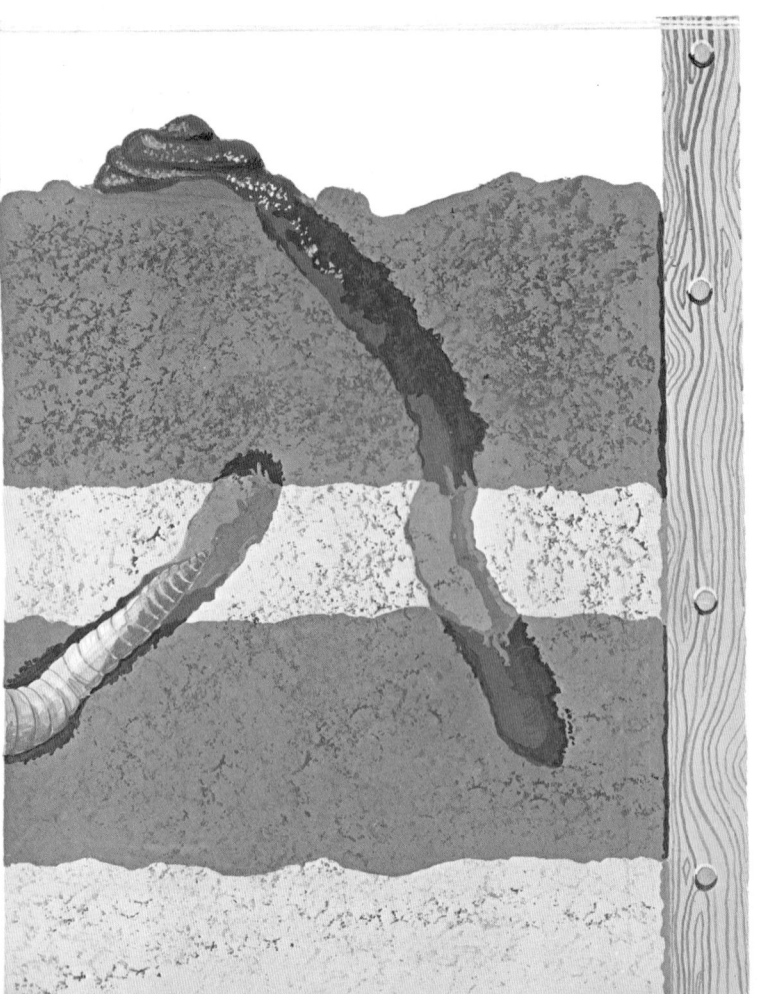

You can watch the patterns your worm makes as it moves through the different colored layers of soil.

Now you can see why worms are so important. They break up big lumps of earth into smaller ones and spread goodness through the soil. The little tunnels they make let air in. Without worms, plants would not be able to grow so well.

Take your worm gently out of its place and put it on a piece of newspaper so you can watch closely how it moves. How does it move? It has hundreds of tiny hairs on its body, which help it grip the soil. It stretches its body in the direction it wants to move, contracts, and then stretches out again. You will see that as it squirms along it seems to make its body fatter and thinner.

When you put your worm back in its box, try giving it a little piece of leaf.

You may find that it uses the leaf to block up the top of its burrow. If the worm were outdoors where it usually lives, this would keep out the cold and draughts.

You should not have your worm visit you for more than two weeks, as it will begin to miss the real earth.

When you put your worm back in the ground, dig a little hole for it and cover it over gently with loose soil. Otherwise a bird might catch it before it has a chance to burrow!

Text copyright © 1980 by Culford Books Limited
Illustrations copyright © 1980 by Judith Allan

All rights reserved. No part of this book may be reproduced or utilized in any form or by any means, electronic or mechanical, including photocopying, recording or by any information storage and retrieval system, without permission in writing from the Publisher. Inquiries should be addressed to Lothrop, Lee & Shepard Books, a division of William Morrow & Company, Inc., 105 Madison Avenue, New York, New York 10016.
First published in the United States of America in 1980.
1 2 3 4 5 6 7 8 9 10

Edited, designed, and produced by Culford Books Limited, 135 Culford Road, London N1, England.
Edited by John Goldsmith.
Designed by Judith Allan.

Printed by Waterlow (Dunstable) Limited, England.

Library of Congress Cataloging in Publication Data

Main entry under title:

It's easy to have a worm visit you.

SUMMARY: Briefly describes the care, feeding, and observation of an earthworm kept in a special home-made container for a short period of time.
1. Earthworms—Juvenile literature. 2. Earthworms as pets—Juvenile literature. [1. Earthworms. 2. Earthworms as pets] I. O'Hagan, Caroline. II. Allan, Judith, (date)
QL391.A6185   595'.146   79-3454
ISBN 0-688-41946-1
ISBN 0-688-51946-6 lib. bdg.

PROPERTY OF
COAL MOUNTAIN ELEM.
CUMMING, GA.